MICROFORMS

The Instructional Media Library

Volume Number 7

MICROFORMS

E. Dale Cluff
Director of Library Services
Southern Illinois University, Carbondale

James E. Duane
Series Editor

Educational Technology Publications
Englewood Cliffs, New Jersey 07632

Library of Congress Cataloging in Publication Data

Cluff, E Dale.
    Microforms.

    (The Instructional media library ; v. no. 7)
    Bibliography: p.
    1. Microforms in education. I. Title. II. Se-
ries: Instructional media library ; v. no. 7.
LB1043.9.C58   371.3'3   80-21457
ISBN 0-87778-167-2

Printed in the United States of America.

Library of Congress Catalog Card Number:
80-21457

International Standard Book Number:
0-87778-167-2

First Printing: January, 1981.

Acknowledgments

Photography and line drawings were done by Carl Buchanan, Microfilm Service Corporation, Salt Lake City, Utah.

Secretarial assistance was given by Dorothy Potter, Marriott Library, University of Utah, Salt Lake City, Utah.

Material in the section on "Local Production" beginning on page 22 has been adapted and reprinted with permission from the *Journal of Micrographics*, Vol. 7, No. 4, March/April 1974. © 1974 National Micrographics Association. ALL RIGHTS RESERVED.

Preface

This book is intended to assist teachers, librarians, and media specialists with integrating microform technology into their instructional strategies. It answers questions related to the availability of information in microform, the acquisition of information in microform, the utilization of microform and related equipment in an educational environment, and the evaluation of this technology.

Each section of the book is self-contained. The Table of Contents and the Glossary will direct the reader to specific aspects of the field.

Though specific equipment, supplies, materials, and companies are mentioned, they are illustrative only. Listing does not necessarily imply endorsement. While those depicted are available mainly in the United States, many microform products are produced in and can be obtained from other countries.

E.D.C.

Table of Contents

MICROFORMS

1.

Introduction

Probably the most famous pigeons in history, at least in the micrographics field, were those which flew between Paris and Bordeaux during the Franco-Prussian War carrying dispatches on microfilm. It is unfortunate that many histories of microfilm begin somewhere around this event because this singular episode in micrographics history has created a perception on the part of some that microforms possess mysterious qualities, are curiosity items, or are only to be used in times of emergency. Nothing could be further from the truth. Microforms play essential roles in our society, in the information industry, the business world, the professions, criminology, preservation, and education.

The educational uses of microforms historically have been in the area of library and information science. Their role in libraries and media centers has been primarily to: (1) save space; (2) acquire materials not otherwise available; (3) retain retrospective volumes instead of binding several issues of hard (paper) copy; (4) preserve deteriorating materials; (5) ease access of bulky materials, such as newspapers; (6) provide working copies of materials too delicate for continual use, such as rare books; (7) save money; (8) acquire materials which would otherwise be difficult to obtain; and (9) reduce mutilation.

The use of microforms by teachers has been a fairly recent phenomenon. The first uses of microforms were in the business field. Suggestions for the use of microforms would naturally be aimed at this group, since that is where the money is. Business people are cost-conscious; so when arguments suggesting reducing stacks of paper, purchasing fewer filing cabinets, saving postage, hiring fewer filers, and reducing space needs were tendered, business people were convinced. But teachers did not jump at the chance to use this medium. One deterrent to the use of microforms in education has been the lack of standardization of both hardware and software. Educators, out of necessity, waited until manufacturers designed equipment which could be used appropriately in the learning process. Software has only recently appeared which could be used to enhance teaching/learning experiences.

2.

Objectives

This book is designed to give the reader the basic knowledge and skills necessary for the proper use of microforms in instruction. Upon completion of the study of this book, the reader should be able to:

1. Describe the physical characteristics of microforms.
2. Enumerate the kinds of information that are most appropriate to put into microform.
3. Locate microforms in libraries.
4. Describe the equipment necessary to use microforms.
5. Use microforms in an educational setting.
6. Understand the advantages and disadvantages of using microforms in instruction.
7. Care for and store microforms and micrographics equipment.
8. Describe the likely future uses of microforms in education.
9. List sources for obtaining microform equipment.
10. List sources for obtaining microform software.

3.

Characteristics of Microforms

Microform is the generic term for micro-images produced in various formats. These images, reduced to a size so small that they cannot be read with the naked eye, may contain textual or graphic information produced by cameras or from digital data by a computer-output recorder. Physically, microforms can be divided into two broad categories of appearance: roll and flat.

Roll microforms are usually 16mm or 35mm wide and are wound on a non-enclosed reel or are loaded into a cartridge or a cassette. Flat microforms are sheets of transparent film (usually four by six inches in size) or opaque paper (of various sizes).

Film used in microform photography is commonly called microfilm. It is usually black and white photographic film with greatly reduced images on it. It consists of a clear, pliable base, coated with material which is photo-sensitive.

The camera negative used for microphotography usually has an emulsion consisting of silver halides, thus giving it the commonly used name of silver film. Silver film is highly sensitive to ordinary light.

After exposure to light, the film has on it a latent image which must be developed chemically to become visible. This image will have tonal values just opposite to those in the object being photographed, so it is called a negative. If a typewritten page is photographed, the negative image will have white letters on a dark background. This camera negative is called a first generation microfilm. When unexposed film is exposed or printed from the camera negative, the image reverses itself and appears on the newly exposed film as positive; or, in other words, the same as the original document being photographed, black letters on white background. This positive film is called a second generation print. This procedure can go on for many generations; however, each successive generation becomes a little poorer in quality.

Micro-images are reduced in size by simply varying the distance of the camera from the item being photographed. Reductions are expressed as a ratio between the size of the object being photographed, which is one, and the proportionate size of the micro-image. For example, a 9 x 12-inch magazine page, photographed at a reduction ratio of 1:12 (or 12X), would form an image on the film 3/4 inch by 1 inch or 1/12 of the linear measure of each dimension.

Formats

Roll microfilm (see Figure 1). The sizes most commonly used in libraries are 16mm and 35mm wide and 100 feet long. Some advantages of this format are:

1. It is heavily used by commercial micropublishers.
2. Many economical microfilm readers which can accommodate this format are readily available.
3. It is easily shelved.
4. Reader/printers are available from which hardcopy prints can be made.
5. This format lends itself to self-service.
6. Distribution is economical.
7. Multiple entries on the same reel remain consistently in the same order.
8. Master copies of this format can be produced economically.

Figure 1

16mm and 35mm roll microfilm

9. Containers in which the reels are housed can be coded for rapid identification of contents.

10. Roll film can be coded to ensure rapid retrieval of specific information on the reel.

11. More people are acquainted with this format, thus necessitating less training.

12. The 35mm width allows a large image area, which is important for the reproduction of newspapers, maps, charts, and other large documents at reasonable reductions.

Some disadvantages of roll microforms are:

1. It is difficult to handle, e.g., threading into a reading device.

2. It is difficult to insert revisions into documents already filmed.

3. It is difficult to make film duplicates of individual documents.

4. Since there is no eye-readable information on the film itself, it is sometimes difficult to insure that the proper reel is placed in the right box.

5. Using one reel of film by one person ties up several other documents which may appear on the same reel.

6. It is costly to distribute individual documents.

Cartridges. A cartridge is a single-core microfilm container which houses 16mm or 35mm roll microfilm. When mounted on a specially designed reader, the film is automatically threaded from the cartridge onto a built-in take-up reel in the reader. During use the film passes from the cartridge to the take-up reel and then must be rewound into the cartridge before it is removed from the reader and reshelved. Cartridges are usually associated with use on a motorized reading device, which speeds access considerably. Cartridges were first used in a major way for access to the catalogs of Sears Roebuck and Company in the late 1950's and early 1960's. They have since been used in libraries for the maintenance of periodical backfiles and card catalogs. Because of the heavy cost of inserting existing reels of film into cartridges, most libraries have not used this particular form of the medium.

Cassettes. A cassette is a double-core microfilm container that encases both a supply and take-up reel in a single unit. Cassettes require no threading of the film and can be removed from the reader at any time without having to be rewound. Microfilm cassettes are as simple to use as a cassette containing sound recordings. Applications of this format of the medium include use with computer-output-microfilm catalogs and serials holdings.

The lack of standardization has slowed the development of both cassette and cartridge applications. In the early 1970's, major microform suppliers offered about 30 different cartridges and cassettes (see Figure 2 for examples), most of them

Figure 2

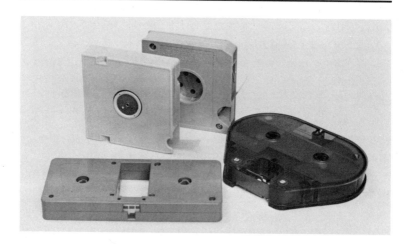

Microfilm in Cassettes and Cartridges

incompatible with each other. The situation has since improved. Cartridges and cassettes protect the film encased in them from fingerprints, but the speed at which the motorized reader passes the film through the system may cause scratches. Readers and reader/printers designed to handle cartridges and cassettes are mechanically complex; hence, they are most costly to purchase and to maintain.

Microfiche (see Figure 3). Microfiche appears as a flat sheet of microfilm ranging in size from 3" x 5" to 6" x 8", with the most common size in use in the United States being 4" x 6". Microfiche in the United States really came into their own in the 1960's and 1970's. Government technical reports were distributed in microfiche format during the 1960's, which provided early impetus to broader use of fiche.

Microfiche is commonly found in libraries and media

Figure 3

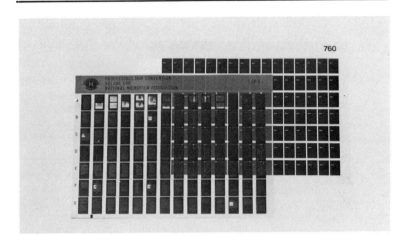

4" x 6" Sheets of Microfiche

centers. At this stage of the development of the medium, there are more applications in the classroom for microfiche than for any other microform. Some of the advantages of microfiche include:

1. They are easy to update.
2. It is easy to obtain hardcopy prints.
3. They are easy and inexpensive to duplicate.
4. The use of one fiche does not tie up other documents.
5. A variety of quality, economical, easy-to-use readers and reader/printers is available.
6. They lend themselves to totally automated retrieval systems.
7. Many microfiche readers are designed to project microfiche images onto large screens for group viewing.

8. Fiche are easy and economical to mail, with no special packing necessary.
9. Secondary distribution is economical.
10. Eye-readable bibliographic information appears on a strip at the top of the fiche for ease of identification.
11. Microfiche readers and the fiche can be coordinately indexed to insure speedy location of information.
12. Much free and inexpensive material from Federal agencies comes in this format.
13. Less training of the patron is required to use microfiche and equipment.
14. The 105mm x 148mm (4" x 6") microfiche is the U.S. and international standard, which facilitates purchase and exchange of the format around the world.
15. It is not difficult to purchase portable readers inexpensively.
16. Fiche lend themselves to innovative uses as information carriers.

Some of the disadvantages of this medium include:

1. Master fiche can be expensive to create.
2. They are easily susceptible to loss or theft.
3. Microfiche are becoming so popular that some micropublishers are publishing in this format in preference to other potentially more suitable microforms.
4. A large microfiche file can be difficult to maintain.
5. Maintaining file integrity is difficult.
6. It is easy to misfile a fiche.
7. It is somewhat of a nuisance, because of the configuration of the images of microfiche, to shift back and forth to obtain the correct image.

Ultrafiche (see Figure 4). A non-standard format occasioned by extremely high reductions, ultrafiche is an efficient storage

Figure 4

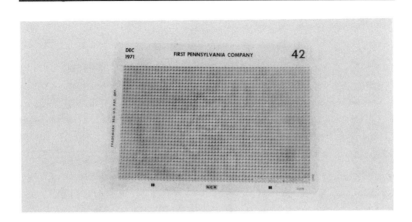

Ultrafiche

Figure 5

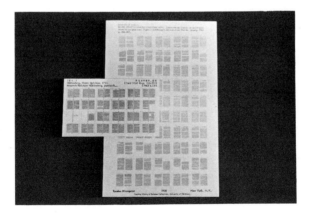

Micro-Opaque

medium. About 1,000 pages of a book can be stored on a 3" x 5" ultrafiche sheet at 90X, reduction ratio, 3,000 pages at 150X. This format was first used as a novelty, but modern ultrafiche developed out of research in optical computer memories. The use of reductions this high in education is questionable. It is highly expensive to produce. It requires special handling, lenses, and reading equipment.

Micro-opaques (see Figure 5). This format is distinguished by paper rather than film micro-image supports. These are identified by their trade names: Microcard, Microprint, Microlex, and Mini-print. Only Microprint is still in production, as a proprietary product of Readex Microprint Corporation. Each microprint is a 6" x 9" card containing up to 100 pages of text in the reduction range of 12X to 24X.

Some of the advantages of micro-opaques include:

1. They offer a unit record approach, which means the use of one opaque does not tie up other documents.
2. They can be stored under the same environmental conditions as books.
3. There is eye-legible information at the top of the card to facilitate ease of identification.

Some disadvantages of micro-opaques are:

1. Opaque to opaque duplicate copies cannot be made.
2. It is difficult to make clear hard copies of micro-opaque images.
3. Special readers and reader/printers are necessary to access the information.
4. Other disadvantages parallel those listed for micro-fiche.

Other microforms. There are other microform formats, but they do not lend themselves as readily to use in education. These include: (1) *Aperture cards.* These are the same size as computer cards and are made of card stock with a slot into which a micro-image is placed, and are used primarily in the data processing industry. They are useful for engineering drawings, maps, etc. (2) *The Jacket card* is a variant of the aperture card containing sleeves for the insertion of 16mm microfilm strips. (3) *Film*, which comes in formats such as chips and strips, is used in systems specifically built to handle these forms.

4.

Types of Information
Most Suitable for Microform

One might say that any document could be microfilmed. Almost any graphic or textual information which can be focused in on by a microfilm camera is suitable for microfilming. However, this generalization must be followed by some qualifications when considering this technology in the educational setting. There are specific documents on microform that are more appropriate than others for use in instruction, given the state-of-the-art.

Newspapers. One of the most useful ways of using microforms is to capture newspapers on either roll microfilm or microfiche. It would be difficult to imagine saving many months' or years' worth of even one daily newspaper in its paper format. The sheer bulk of these papers would quickly eat up valuable storage space, not to mention the disadvantage of having yellowing, deteriorating pages to read. Also, the larger the stack grew, the more difficult it would be to locate the desired issue.

Microforms solve such problems nicely. With proper indexing, it is simple to retrieve the exact date and page needed. The space to store the microform copy is a fraction of that required to store the paper copy. Deterioration and dirty hands and clothes are not a concern with microform.

Nearly all major U.S. and foreign newspapers are available

in microform. Geographic regions of the U.S. are represented by micropublished editions of titles such as *The New York Times, Wall Street Journal, Washington Post, Houston Post, Chicago Times,* and *Los Angeles Times.* Many foreign newspapers also are available.

Micropublishers perform valuable services, one of which is to preserve newspapers published about special aspects of our society or history. Samples of special newspaper collections include: *Newspapers of the American Civil War, Early American Newspapers, Newspapers from the Black Community, Newspapers Along America's Great Trails, The Depression Years—1929-1938, The Underground Press,* and *Contemporary Newspapers of the North American Indian.* (All of the above are products of the Micro Photo Division of Bell & Howell.)

Magazines. Thousands of periodical titles are available in microform. It can be advantageous to acquire backfiles of popular and scholarly journals and magazines in this format. The advantages include space and binding savings and deterring mutilation. Some libraries subscribe to current issues of periodicals in the paper copy and then receive the entire year's worth on microform instead of binding the paper copy. Often, this can be less costly than pulling all of the individual issues off the shelf at the end of the year, checking to see if they are all in good conditior, sending them to a commercial bindery, waiting for them to return, labeling them, and finally shelving them.

Subscribing to the microform annual cumulation of periodicals is generally less costly than subscribing to two copies of a magazine. Some libraries have the practice of holding one copy back to be used as a binding copy because the use the title receives leaves the public copy in such poor condition at the end of the year that it is in no condition to bind. Some micropublishers offer subscriptions to periodicals in several formats: hard (paper) copy or microfiche or roll microfilm (open reel, cartridge, or cassette). Some libraries acquire individual issues of certain titles only on microform, never receiving the paper copy.

Collections. An interesting and valuable technique some micropublishers use is to gather together information on a subject, microfilm it, and then make it available as a collection. These collections are attractive to larger libraries or special libraries because it saves considerable time and money to acquire a ready-made collection than to locate each individual title and pay for the paper volumes. Schools can usually borrow, on an interlibrary loan basis, materials from neighboring college, university, and special libraries. A few examples of microform collections include: *French Political Pamphlets, John Brown's Letters,* and *Early English Courtesy Books* (available from Micro Photo Division of Bell & Howell). Other collections include: *Crime and Juvenile Delinquency, The Indian Rights Association Papers, Books About North American Indians on Microfilm,* and *Perspectives on American Labor* (available from Microfilming Corporation of America).

Out-of-print and costly materials. Micropublishing fills an important need when it comes to obtaining information which may be out-of-print or too costly to acquire in paper format. Many books of this nature are available in microform thanks to the efforts of some micropublishers. One notable example of this is the *Books on Demand* program of University Microfilms International (UMI). They maintain a list of well over 100,000 out-of-print titles. Upon receipt of an order, UMI will make prints of the pages of the book, bind it, and ship it to the customer for a nominal price. UMI and other micropublishers provide the service of locating the needed book if it is not on their current list, microfilming it, and making it available. Once a microform copy is made of an item and a master copy retained, the item is no longer really "out of print."

Government publications. Another appropriate and valuable way microform technology is assisting the transfer of information is in the area of U.S.A. and international publications. An often overlooked resource on the part of the researcher is this large field of publishing. Much information is generated by U.S.A. and foreign governments. Every state has several libraries acting as official selective depositories for U.S. Government documents. Since there is so much published by the Government Printing Office (GPO) and foreign countries, many micropublishers microfilm the paper documents and make them available in microform. The GPO itself also distributes some of its publications in this format. Some documents published by GPO are available to the public, libraries, and schools free of charge; others can be obtained from GPO at a nominal fee. This, plus the breadth of subjects covered by the GPO, makes the use of these microforms in education very attractive.

Other materials. Some information is valuable but is never published in hard copy. Much of this is made available, however, through the medium of microform. Examples of this type of information include:

1. *Theses and dissertations.* Graduate students across the nation turn out thousands of these annually. Some represent excellent research and are a valuable resource. These were virtually inaccessible and unavailable unless one knew of the student's work, until University Microfilms International (UMI) began their project. Through an active and intensive acquisitions and indexing program, UMI now has available on microfilm most dissertations written.

2. *Educational material.* Providing access to educational literature, the Educational Resources Information Center (ERIC) was established in the mid-1960's. Decentralized centers called "clearinghouses" are located across the country in organizations whose primary goal is some aspect of education. The ERIC collections of research reports, study

reports, papers presented at professional meetings, special reports, etc., are made available for a small fee in either hard copy or microfiche. Many libraries and educational agencies subscribe to the ERIC microfiche collection, which is indexed in a monthly abstracting journal called *Research in Education*. An *ERIC Thesaurus* is the authority for subject terms in the ERIC system.

3. *Human Relations Area Files.* The *Human Relations Area Files (HRAF)* is a collection of primary source materials (mainly published books and articles, but including some unpublished manuscripts) on selected cultures or societies representing most areas of the world. The materials are organized and filed by a method designed for the rapid and accurate retrieval of specific data on given cultures and topics. File materials can be useful for students of anthropology, sociology, geography, politics, psychology, and such diverse fields as literature, home economics, art, and agricultural development. Wider distribution of the *HRAF Files* was made possible by the development in 1958 of the *HRAF Microfiles,* which are produced on 4" x 6" microfiche.

4. *Archives and manuscripts.* Much material is collected by individuals and libraries which may be of local value or have highly specialized interest. These materials consist mainly of letters, notebooks, journals, handbills, posters, early drafts of articles and books, etc. This material, often one of a kind, is sometimes microfilmed and distributed by the owning institution via this medium. Some micropublishers have obtained rights to do the microfilming and then sell copies of some of the high-interest items.

5.

Acquiring Materials in Microform

Criteria for selecting a micropublication for the library or the instructional process should differ little from criteria used to select other library and instructional resources. The relevance of the item to the educational objective is of utmost importance. This is followed by the physical quality of the format and whether there is appropriate associated equipment available to effectively use the microform.

Commercial sources. There are standard works which are indispensable when it comes to locating, evaluating, and acquiring information on microform. *Subject Guide to Microforms in Print* and *Guide to Microforms in Print* (Westport, CT: Microform Review, Inc.) are "cumulative annual listings of microform titles, comprising books, journals, newspapers, government publications, archival material, collections and other projects, etc., which are currently available from micropublishing organizations throughout the world." These handy guides give price, availability, format, and bibliographic information. The *Micropublishers' Trade List Annual* (Microform Review, Inc.) includes microphotographed copies of actual catalogs and brochures of micropublishers, worldwide. To illustrate the magnitude of this work, the 1978 edition included over 14,000 pages from hundreds of catalogs and brochures. *Microform Review,* a professional journal containing articles dealing with microforms, has lengthy reviews of micropublications, previews of forthcoming publications, and a listing of recent microform projects.

Local production. Considerable flexibility is offered when locally producing microform presentations. Probably the best format to use in this process is microfiche. Microfiche lends itself well to this application because it is laid out logically, can be easily indexed both internally and externally, and is easy to handle.

Microfiche is laid out in grid fashion. The number of image spaces on each fiche is determined by the magnification used in the photographic and readback process. One standard is a 98-grid fiche, which usually requires a 24X lens to bring the image back to normal, readable size.

When producing your own fiche, draw a layout sheet which corresponds to the number of image areas desired in the finished fiche (see Figure 6). Be sure to leave a strip of space at the top of the grid for the purpose of affixing eye-readable information. This information might include filing, classification, and identification data.

As you identify which material goes into each space (in other words, the sequence of the information), mark a number, working from left to right and top to bottom, on the original and on the paper layout. This process is critical, as it will instruct the cameraperson as to the sequence of the presentation. For example, you are going to convert a set of slides of biological specimens to microfiche. Place the slides in the order you want them to appear on the fiche, number them consecutively, and then number the spaces in the layout sheet to match the numbers on the slides. The next step is to send the set of slides and the layout sheet to a company which can photographically convert the slides to a master microfiche. Any number of copies of the master can then be made for distribution.

To make a master fiche from materials other than slides, a similar process is used. Let us say you want to produce a lesson using charts, graphs, and text.

Figure 6

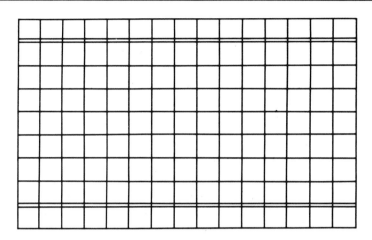

Layout Sheet for Use When Producing Fiche

1. Prepare the material on normal letter-size paper. Each sheet of paper will become a frame in the finished product. A regular type font is adequate, but a primary typewriter using all capital letters produces a fine finished image. Draw charts and graphs in dark inks or paints for clear contrast. Headings on these can be typed, put on with transfer letters, or hand printed. Pictures or clipped material can be placed on the paper with double-sided tape, paste, or spray adhesive.

2. Decide the sequence and determine the layout. Using a schematic of a blank fiche, referred to earlier, determine the sequence for the graphic and textual material. Next, number the sheets of paper in order of presentation, then place the same numbers in the schematic of the blank fiche in the desired sequence. The number of spaces in the fiche will dictate how much information can be placed on it. If only a few frames are needed, this leaves the flexibility of using

every other frame, or placing more than one unit on a fiche, or of using the remainder of the fiche for other purposes, such as reference material, teacher notes, etc. If more frames are needed, a second fiche can be used to continue the presentation. Be sure to dedicate the top portion of the fiche to eye-readable information.

3. Film the material. This can be done by:

a. Sending the material out to a company which can photographically convert the original material to a microform master. This technique will be used by teachers whose schools do not have filming equipment.

b. Filming the material yourself. If you or a member of the library/media center staff have the expertise and have access to the appropriate equipment, doing the filming can be a rewarding experience. A step and repeat camera or a planetary camera will do the job. With the appropriate size film in the camera, the original material is then exposed on the film in the proper sequence.

4. Copies of the master fiche can then be produced on regular microfiche duplicating equipment.

Another technique of creating the master fiche is to use a jacket system as an interim step from original to final product. This system allows the opportunity to update the material or change sequence. This is done by making photographic images of the original material, then cutting the film into strips or single exposed units. You then slip the pieces of film into sleeves on a blank jacketed fiche in the appropriate sequence. Distribution copies are then made from this master negative. If the sequence of the presentation is changed, the film images in the jacketed fiche may be rearranged and another master negative created without the necessity of redoing the photographic work.

6.

Locating Microform Information
in Libraries

There is considerable inconsistency in the way microforms are treated bibliographically in libraries. In some libraries each book, media material, and microform is fully cataloged and classified and the cataloging data placed in the library's main catalog. Hence, when seeking information, a library patron may find the item regardless of the form in which the information comes. Appropriate notes in the cataloging data identify the format so that the proper equipment can be called upon to access the information.

Other libraries give full cataloging to a single microform book but not to a collection of microform books. These are often left intact as a collection, and a few generic headings which describe the collection are included in the library's catalog. Often, a microform collection is accompanied by a printed index which is given full cataloging. The patron then must find the index and use it as a guide to individual items in the collection. Examples of these indexes include: *American Fiction 1774-1900; Cumulative Author Index to the Microfilm Collection* (New Haven, Conn.: Research Publications, Inc., 1974); *Russian Revolutionary Literature Collection, Houghton Library, Harvard University—A Descriptive Guide and Key to the Collection on Microfilm* (New Haven, Conn.: Research Publications, Inc., 1976); *The Microbook Library of American Civilization, Author Catalog* (Chicago:

Library Resources, Inc., 1971); and *Microfilm Edition of the Papers of Daniel Webster—Guide and Index to the Microfilm* (Ann Arbor, Michigan: University Microfilms, 1971).

Some libraries have special lists or catalogs dedicated to microform holdings. These are useful when trying to locate specific items, as you are not required to sift through entries for books and A-V materials. These special lists are usually maintained at or near the reference desk.

When looking for information in microform, be persistent. The library is likely to have what you want, but because of the "nature of the beast," it may be difficult to find a clear trail which will lead to exactly what you desire. Don't hesitate to ask the librarian or media specialist for assistance. The trail, though long, may be well worth the effort.

7.

Microform Equipment

Micro-images must be enlarged to be read by the naked eye. A microform reader is the basic device for accomplishing this. It is done through the use of light, lenses, and mirrors. There are several different sizes and shapes of readers, in varying degrees of complexity, on the market. They range in size from a small handheld unit similar to a magnifying glass (see Figure 7) to large table-top models weighing 40-60 pounds. They range in complexity from those having no moving parts to motorized units. These range in cost from just a few dollars to over a thousand dollars. The librarian and the teacher should select the reader which will best accommodate the micro-forms in the collection and help to accomplish the educational goals.

Readers

Microform reading machines (samples pictured in Figures 8 through 13) are usually manufactured to perform a specific function. For example, a roll microfilm reader will best accommodate roll microfilm; a microfiche reader will enable one to read a microfiche; a microcard reader will handle opaque cards, etc. Some microform equipment manufacturers have tried, with little success, to design microform readers which will accommodate two or more formats of microform.

Figure 7

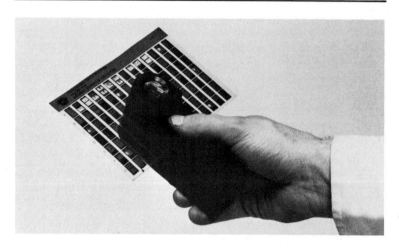

Handheld Microfiche Reader (Criterion)

Usually it is better to obtain single-function, simple-to-use readers. Those microform readers which are designed to accommodate more than one type of microform are generally more expensive initially, are more complicated, and require more upkeep.

For individual study, it is probably better to obtain inexpensive, yet durable, easy-to-use, table-top readers. For group instruction, readers with projection capabilities should be acquired.

Since the acquisition of microform-reading machines represents a major investment for schools and libraries, and since there is a wide variety of microform readers from which to choose, a list of desirable characteristics of microform readers may be useful.

1. The screen should be large enough to hold the full text (page) of the original.

Figure 8

Portable Microfilm Reader (Realist Swinger)

Figure 9

Roll Film Reader (Canon 320)

2. For clarity of image, the entire screen should be uniformly clear.

3. The screen should be uniformly bright.

4. At least a 90° image rotation capability is necessary.

5. Simplicity of operation is essential. All controls should be labeled and easily accessible from a seated position.

6. Ruggedness of construction is necessary. The reader must be able to endure everyday use. Controls, especially gears, should be made of high-quality materials.

7. The screen or viewing angle should correspond as nearly as possible to a normal reading position. Travel of head and eye should be horizontal rather than vertical.

8. The screen should have a non-glare surface. Be cautious of tinted screens, since tint can distort the hue of color microforms.

Figure 10

Roll Film Reader (Kodak MPE)

---

9. The controls should move easily and smoothly.

10. The reader should focus smoothly without being jumpy. When advancing from frame to frame, the screen image should stay in focus.

11. Film loading and unloading should be easy.

12. The machine should be constructed in such a way that it will sit stably without being easily tipped over.

13. The lamp in the reader should have a reasonable life expectancy, and access to the lamp should be easy.

14. An adequate cooling system for the reader is important.

15. The glass flats which hold the film in place should be separable and easily removed for cleaning.

16. All accessories should be attached to the machine. Parts should be easily accessible for cleaning and repair. The parts should be easily obtainable from commercial sources.

Figure 11

Portable Microfiche Reader (Realist Executive)

17. Simple, well-illustrated, attractive operating instructions should be provided.

18. Screen material should be shatterproof.

19. Whether fixed or variable magnification, it should be compatible with the microforms in the school's collections.

20. When film is advancing in a roll machine, it should be done smoothly and with no danger of damaging the film.

21. A reasonable warranty should accompany the machine. It should also be relatively easy to service.

22. When in use, the reader should create a minimum of noise from the operation of fans and motors.

There are a few valuable sources for evaluating microform reading equipment. Some of the sources themselves contain evaluative statements about the equipment, some report specifications about equipment without including evaluations, and some list guidelines on how to purchase equipment.

Figure 12

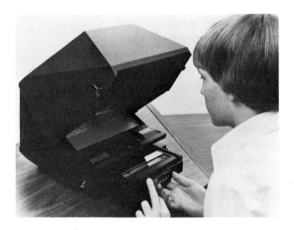

Portable Microfiche Reader (Realist FP 11)

Perhaps the most useful source for librarians and educators for information about the evaluation of equipment is the American Library Association's *Library Technology Reports.* The "Microform and Equipment" section provides periodic reports, based on tests, on any microform equipment a library or school is likely to buy. The machines are given an impartial evaluation.

A relatively new periodical titled *Microform Equipment Review* (Microform Review, Inc.) is also a useful tool.

A self-help evaluation source is William R. Hawken's work, *Evaluating Microfiche Readers: A Handbook for Librarians* (Council on Library Resources, 1975).

A valuable standard source for microform hardware specifications is the *Guide to Micrographic Equipment.* Published by the National Microfilm Association (NMA), it is updated with new editions regularly.

Figure 13

Left: Microfiche Reader (NMI 75)
Right: Portable Microfiche Reader (Realist FP 11)

The media specialist in concert with the teacher can help familiarize students with microform equipment and train them in its use. As with any audio or visual equipment, a student can become dissatisfied quickly if frustration and embarrassment result from the inability to competently operate reading machines.

Most microform reading equipment manufacturers supply operating instructions with their readers in booklet or pamphlet form. In addition, some companies provide simple operating instructions on the reader itself.

If readers are acquired which do not have adequate instructions on them, these can be added by school personnel. The media specialist and art/graphics faculty can work together to create nicely illustrated, easy-to-follow machine-use instructions. They can be painted or adhered to the reader in any number of useful ways.

It cannot be stressed too much that for students to feel comfortable with this medium, they must be trained. The investment in training time at the beginning of the school term will pay big dividends later.

Reader/Printers

A reader/printer (Figures 14 and 15) is a machine used for both viewing and producing occasional hard (paper) copy reproductions from microforms. At least one reader/printer should be provided for all but the smallest collections. Large libraries with substantial numbers of microform publications and an array of microform formats will need several.

There will probably always be a demand for paper copies of microform articles. The type of microform collection the school has will determine the degree of demand for hard copies. When only a few copies of a document are needed, a low-cost, low-volume reader/printer may suffice. When many copies are needed, a high-volume unit may be required.

Several processes are used by reader/printer manufacturers to produce enlarged paper copies of micro-images. While most of the processes produce a useful print, they vary considerably as to cost, characteristics, quality, and printing time. Most printing processes use coated paper in either roll or sheet form. The cost of supplies varies from manufacturer to manufacturer.

Most of the characteristics desired for microform readers also apply to reader/printers. There are some additional characteristics, however, for reader/printers. Some of these are highlighted below:

1. Clarity of print. This depends partly, of course, upon the quality and condition of the microform from which the print is being made.

2. Contrast.

3. Ease of use. While it is desirable to allow the user to operate the machine, it might be necessary to obtain a

Figure 14

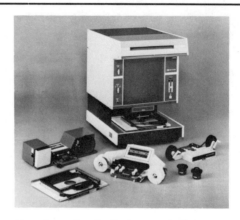

Microform Reader/Printer with Fiche, Roll,
and Cartridge Adapters (Minolta 405)

Figure 15

Microfiche Reader/Printer (Canon 370)

machine which is slightly more difficult to operate and allow only staff to make the copies. This option may produce better copies with less waste.

4. Polarity of the print. Most users prefer to read positive print, e.g., black print on white background. Many reader/printers reverse the polarity, that is, a copy from a negative film will be positive and vice versa. Other reader/printers are designed not to reverse. In these machines, a positive image film will turn out a positive image print. Machines are available which, by a flip of a switch, will operate either in a reversible or non-reversible mode.

The number of reader/printers to obtain is a difficult matter to determine. Certainly it is desirable to have at least one for each type of microform (roll film, fiche, opaque) in a medium-sized library. Beyond that, the volume of printing business will be the biggest determinant. A few libraries have chosen to buy only reader/printers and not readers. This gives the user the advantage of remaining at one place and not having to reinsert the microform into another piece of equipment, relocate the desired image, and then obtain the print. Cost and convenience are major factors in determining the number of reader/printers to obtain.

Duplicators

Some institutions possessing large microform collections have elected to provide another dimension to their microform services: duplicating. This service provides the ability to make fiche-to-fiche duplicates. Very few libraries are providing film-to-film duplicates at this time. With some fiche-to-fiche duplicators, a segment of a roll of film can also be duplicated if needed. Again, need for this service is dictated by several factors. The major factor is whether or not the microfiche collection circulates. If file integrity is a major concern, then a duplicating system is most useful. With a duplicating system, the school's fiche copy stays, while the duplicated copy leaves the building.

Figure 16

Microfiche Duplicator (Canon 360H and 480 VC)

The sophistication of the system will be determined by the volume of business this service will generate. Most libraries will probably not have a need for a large, high-production duplicator costing many thousands of dollars and capable of producing thousands of fiche per day. More appropriate is probably a small, low-volume duplicator costing between $300 and $3,000, which is basically manually operated, is used occasionally, and is not intended for long production runs (see Figure 16).

One final consideration related to duplicators and reader/printers is their location in relation to the microform themselves and to the microform readers. There are certainly different options open to the school. System and user needs should dictate the location of this equipment.

Preventive Maintenance

There seems to be a reluctance on the part of the novice to use a piece of machinery the first time. If directed to a machine which is malfunctioning, the first-time users, and sometimes even the initiated, may be intimidated to the point of leaving, never to return to try again; or, to be more realistic, they may leave but be very reluctant to return and try again. To avoid this unpleasant circumstance, a standard checklist for inspection of microform machines can be created. Each type of machine has its own specialized characteristics, but all machines have some common parts which should be inspected regularly. Daily, staff should:

1. Turn the machine on. This insures the proper working of the on/off switch, the light bulb, and the electrical system. (Note: Some bulbs can be damaged if touched with bare hands. A light cloth or glove should be used when changing bulbs.)

2. Briefly operate the moving parts. This includes the crank for some machines, moving the carrier on others, activating the motorized advance, etc.

3. Check lenses, glass plates, screens, and mirrors for excess dust, marks, cracks, chips, or breaks.

Any machine found to be malfunctioning, for whatever reason, should be repaired immediately or removed from the public area until it is repaired and placed back in service. If a machine is removed for repair, it is preferable to replace it with a back-up unit if one is available. If there is no back-up unit, it is acceptable to leave an empty study station. It is better for a microform user to see an empty space and be required to walk a few feet to a serviceable machine than to sit down at a malfunctioning piece of equipment. If the machine is too large to move, an "out of order" sign should be placed on it in a prominent place as soon as possible after discovery of the malfunction. Then see that it is repaired quickly.

A regular cleaning schedule for all microform equipment should be established, as improperly maintained equipment can result in damage to microforms. A staff member should be assigned to systematically clean each piece of equipment. The frequency should be dictated by the maintenance manual for the specific piece of equipment and by experience in the environment in which the equipment is housed. The physical environment plays a major role in determining how frequently equipment should be cleaned. The degree of environmental control varies between buildings. This environment ranges from relatively dust free to highly contaminated. Appropriate cleaning materials should be used, as recommended by the manuals for each piece of equipment. If cleaning information is not readily available, a good rule of thumb is to use a camel-hair brush, non-abrasive cloth, or tissue and mild cleaning agents. This is especially critical when cleaning mirrors, screens, and glass parts.

Generally, the more complex a machine, the greater the likelihood that it will need frequent repair and the less likely a regular staff member will be able to accomplish the repair. It might be less costly to purchase a maintenance contract for selected pieces of microform equipment. When thinking about and negotiating for a maintenance contract, the following should be considered:

1. Complexity of the machine.
2. Amount of use given the machine.
3. Amount of dysfunction caused when the machine is down.
4. Maintenance and repair expertise of school personnel.
5. Cost of training a staff member to provide the necessary maintenance and repair.
6. The proximity of the company providing maintenance and repair service to the school.
7. Hours during the week the service is provided by the contracting agency.

8. Skill of service personnel.
9. Cost of the contract.
10. The types of maintenance, repair work, and parts guaranteed by the contract.

Most companies with whom a maintenance contract agreement has been made will respond quickly to a service call. Hence, the piece of equipment will not have to remain "down" for long periods of time. Typical microform equipment which might be considered for a service contract are reader/printers, duplicators, and heavily used motorized readers.

8.

Care and Storage of Microforms

Microform hardware and software should be given the same consideration as other media hardware and software when it comes to care and storage. They should be handled in such a way that wear and damage is kept to a minimum, and they should be stored in clean surroundings. The temperature and moisture content of the air should remain as moderate as possible. Extreme heat and moisture can damage microforms. When not in use, microform equipment should be covered with dust covers to protect lenses, mirrors, glass plates, and moving parts. Care should be taken that the equipment is placed on firm, roomy surfaces to minimize chances of being knocked to the floor. Hardware should be inspected upon receipt to insure that no parts are broken or malfunctioning. If something is wrong, bring it to the attention of the manufacturer.

Care

Microforms themselves should be inspected upon receipt. If there are too many for a thorough inspection of each roll or sheet, then a spot-check would be sufficient. If, however, manageable numbers are involved, each item should be inspected. It is helpful to wear white, lint-free gloves when inspecting microforms. Ideally, inspection should occur as soon as possible after the microforms are received and before any identifying marks are placed on them or their containers. Any microform found to be unacceptable should be returned to the supplier immediately. Things to look for during inspection include:

1. Does the container (box, envelope) house exactly what the label on the container says?
2. Are there any visible tears, wrinkles, or blotches on the film?
3. Are there visible water marks on the container or film?
4. Are there eye-readable headers on the film indicating what is on the film?
5. Are any fiche or rolls missing?
6. Are any pages missing?
7. Are the images on the screen clear?

Film which has been heavily used becomes dirty. Roll microfilm and microfiche can be satisfactorily cleaned with a non-toxic cleaning solvent and lint-proof cloths.

Roll film which has been torn in use can be spliced just like a filmstrip or motion picture film. The media center should have on hand 16mm and 35mm splicers and materials.

Storage

Before getting into specific types of storage equipment, a few general observations should be made. The type of filmstock to be stored, and the use to which it will be put, will determine the storage environment and facilities best suited to a given school's microform information system.

In addition to temperature, humidity, and air purity conditions, other factors should be considered.

1. Microfilm, either for use or archival storage, should be protected from physical or chemical damage by placing it in containers which are free of acid, sulphur, and peroxide.

2. Specially designed filing cabinets are available for 16mm and 35mm film boxes, various sizes of microfiche, and

jackets. Shelving is also available for roll microfilm containers.

3. The storage cabinets should be constructed with steel, well covered by inert paint, or with stainless steel or aluminum.

4. Films should be stored high enough to avoid possible water damage.

5. Tightly packed films are less affected by either fire or humidity than are loosely packed films.

6. Acid from skin deteriorates silver film, so care should be exercised to handle the film only at its edges.

We must distinguish between the type of film generally stored in archives and the type stored in libraries and media centers. Master microfilm copies or camera negatives are generally stored with the utmost care in archival storage conditions. Most libraries and schools do not possess master copies; rather, they use copies made from the master or intermediate copies.

Now, we turn to the various storage options. Roll film, whether 16mm or 35mm, is stored in the following ways.

1. Slide drawer metal cabinets (see Figure 17). These vary in price, dimensions, number of drawers, number of trays per drawer, and in storage capacity. They are manufactured and distributed by a number of companies. A selective list of the companies is at the back of this book. These types of cabinets offer the advantage of protection from dust and dirt.

2. Space-saver cabinets. These are usually placed on top of a base unit. Either left- or right-hand models with four vertical drawers, each with six shelves, are offered. This concept offers greater floor space utilization.

3. Regular library shelves. This method is not recommended, as use of space is not efficient and boxes can be pushed out of sight to the rear of the shelf.

4. Roll film shelving (see Figure 18). Standard roll microfilm shelving is now available from most equipment suppliers.

Figure 17

Roll Film Filing Cabinet

Figure 18

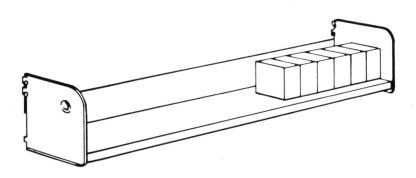

*Roll Film Shelving for Use in
Standard Library Stacks*

Interchangeable with any metal library bookshelf, the roll film shelf features a vertical inset four inches from the front, designed to keep the film storage box aligned with the edge of the shelf for orderly display and ready visibility of titles.

5. Adapted library shelving. Some schools have locally adapted standard seven-inch library shelves by using wood or metal and creating a shallow shelf to cause the same effect as the shelf mentioned in (4) above. Some of these have been adapted to allow for two-tier stacking of roll microfilm. This design is often used when shelving film along with regular books and periodicals; thus, better space utilization is accomplished.

6. Another shelf-type arrangement involves shelves 18 inches deep. These shelves are placed in ranges with 14 shelves per section. Then seven specially designed cardboard containers 18 inches long and the width of a roll microfilm storage box are placed side by side on the shelves. Ten boxes of film are placed in each cardboard storage container, thus allowing 70 reels of film to be stored on each 36" x 18" shelf. This is an inexpensive, space-efficient method (see Figure 19).

7. Another method not often seen is the Carousel filing system. This system is usually designed for cartridge film, either roll or sheet. These vary in size and complexity from desk-top, single-tiered, manually controlled units to many-tiered, motor driven units several feet in diameter.

Microfiche are stored in a number of ways.

1. Slide drawer metal cabinets (see Figure 20). These are by far the most commonly used microfiche storage method. These come in sizes similar to the roll film cabinets and can be obtained from the same suppliers. They vary somewhat in the features offered but are fairly standard. These also come in space-saving vertical units.

2. Other methods. Some other interesting but highly tailored-to-a-specific-use systems are in use: racks with hanging files, specially designed desk-top boxes or boxes to

Figure 19

Another Shelf-Type System for Shelving Roll Film

Figure 20

Microfiche Filing Cabinet

be placed on shelves, loose-leaf pages with slots in which the fiche rest, hardcopy books with pages of fiche, etc.

9.

Educational Uses of Microforms

The earliest use of microforms in schools can be traced back to the 1950's, when some innovative school administrators converted papercopy student records to microform to help solve space problems and to maintain the records securely. About the same time, some school media specialists and librarians envisioned being able, through the purchase of newspapers and magazines on microfilm, to expand and preserve library resources, save space, and, at the same time, save dollars.

The mid-sixties saw microforms used for instructional purposes. These programs, initially funded by the Federal Government, spread across the United States. They cut across urban and rural areas and touched all grade levels although, historically, most applications were at the elementary level.

No single approach to teaching contains all of the answers. Using different approaches offers the advantage of possibly reaching more students. When preparing any instructional materials, the preparation should follow closely the principles of learning applicable to those objectives which will meet student needs.

School children readily accept microforms, since they have grown up with television and other visual media. Many children are familiar with the operation of motion picture and filmstrip projectors as well as with audio- and videocassette players and recorders. A roll film or fiche reader is no more complicated than these.

In the few short years microforms have been used in education on the elementary and secondary levels, definite advantages have been observed. These can be generally summarized as follows:

1. Microforms are an excellent way of expanding and enhancing existing resources with primary source materials.

2. These expanded resources offer more opportunity for individual research possibilities.

3. Primary resources bring immediacy of the event to the student.

4. Students, through the study of these resources, learn how to evaluate sources. They can become "experts" in specific areas.

5. Microforms offer versatility. In one format, the written word, pictorial information, graphic presentations, exercises, and computer information can be stored and recalled.

6. Because of this versatility, the microform reader can substitute for slide and filmstrip projectors, textbooks, journals, workbooks, and programmed learning machines.

7. Microforms ease storage problems.

8. They eliminate lost issues or mutilated pages of magazines and newspapers.

9. Microforms are easily transported.

10. They are inexpensive to mail.

User Reactions

As with any technology, attitudes on the part of the user are of the utmost importance. Attitudes are usually a direct result of the training one has to enable him or her to comfortably use the hardware and software. If not thoroughly oriented and well-trained, the first-time user of microforms will most likely become intimidated. Only the persistent will keep trying until the system is mastered. But almost anyone, even grade schoolers, given adequate training and introduction to this medium, can soon feel at home.

When considering microforms and related equipment for purchase, human factors should be considered in addition to the technical aspects listed in another part of this book. When engaged in individual study, people want to be as comfortable as possible. The slant of the screen will dictate head position. The evenness of light projecting the image, the polarity of the microform, and the brightness of the light will affect reader comfort. The height of the reader in relation to the seating position of the user will dictate body comfort. The placement of the controls on the machine affects arm and hand comfort.

If the user is in a comfortable position, the light is right, and the reader is easy to use, there is no noticeable difference in the fatigue factor when doing prolonged reading of microforms than when reading hardcopy books, newspapers, or magazines. In fact, some people prefer reading the microform copy of bulky items such as computer printouts, newspapers, and folio-size monographs.

Use Environment

Another important factor when using microform technology in education is the environment in which it is used. The most useable microform equipment may be available and the user may be well-trained, but if the place where the student will use the technology is poorly designed, user satisfaction will be low. The place where the microforms are stored when not in use should be well lighted, easily accessible, and close to the use area. The tables or work surfaces on which the readers are placed should be at a height suitable to the size of the users and large enough for notetaking. Ambient light in relation to the brightness of the image on the screen is important. Many microform readers can be used by individuals in normal room illumination. As with most projection devices, however, care should be taken to avoid direct light on the screen. Nor is it wise to place the reader in front of a window in a position where the user is facing the glare of the light coming in the window. When using a microform reader as a projector, the room should be darkened in the same manner as though slides or a movie were being shown. It goes without saying that a room in which microform viewing occurs must have a sufficient number of electrical outlets. The software and the hardware ought to be as close to each other as possible, thus reducing the amount of travel and disturbance which could take place if the two were some distance from each other.

If all microform study or use is done in the school library or media center, the materials, the equipment, and the space set-up should be ready before the students arrive for the learning experience. Then, during the experience, care should be taken to insure minimal disruption by other students, phones, noisy machines, etc.

Specific Teaching Applications

Individualized instruction. Thus far, the most widespread use of microforms in education has been for individual study. From elementary grades to adult education, administrators, librarians, and teachers have seen the potential and are using microforms regularly in this application. Microforms are especially suited to individualized instruction for the following reasons:

1. A school can enrich its library or classroom collection of learning materials substantially, usually at less cost than with hardcopy counterparts. Many excellent collections and individual works on various subjects designed for specific grade or achievement level can be acquired from micropublishers. These can be used either for quick reference or sustained reading or study.

2. With these materials which extend the existing re-

sources of the school, individual student interest may be satisfied and students can progress at their own rate. This is especially important for mentally gifted students who are well ahead of the rest of the class and who must remain challenged if boredom is to be prevented.

3. One-on-one peer instruction is ideal using microforms. With the image of the page in front of the student, the peer-tutor knows exactly which page the student is on, and with the print somewhat larger than that of the original, reference can be made easily to a specific word, group of words, diagram, etc.

4. Using microforms, a student's hands are free to take notes, to give written response to instructions or questions in the work, or to simply prop his or her head or hold an object.

5. Microforms are so light and of such a convenient size that they are very mobile. This means students can easily carry them from one study area to another as need dictates. Movement of individual study materials from classroom to library to other classrooms can be done with little disruption of continuity.

6. Microforms can be used as inexpensive group supplementary materials. In other words, a student can own or borrow for a long time a reproduction of materials which are used in a group teaching situation. This allows for frequent review and study on one's own time.

7. Programmed instruction is another application to which microforms lend themselves. They can range from a microfiche carrying the complete learning program, to a microform being used in conjunction with another medium, to a multimedia package. Used as a self-contained program, a microfiche can have the information so arranged that a student can move from one frame to another in any of four directions (left, right, up, or down). This facilitates following different paths on the fiche in typical programmed instruction style (see Figure 21).

Figure 21

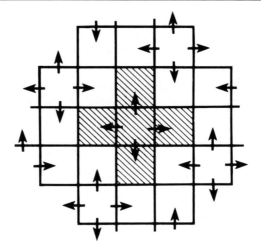

*Microfiche offers the versatility of moving
from one image to others above, below, or to either side.*

Group instruction. An educational application of micro-forms which is just coming into its own is small-group and large-group instruction. For small groups, one machine can be used with a few students clustered around it. One machine projecting an image on a screen or a large sheet of paper on a table works nicely, or a few students can have their own reader, each looking at the same material. In the latter example, a teacher can divide the class into four or five equal-sized groups and assign the same material to each, requiring a report from each group.

For large-group instruction, the material may be projected on a large screen or on a rear screen system in the classroom. If the right type of microform reader is acquired, it can be used either for large groups by removing the screen from it and allowing the image to project onto a larger screen, or for individual instruction by leaving the screen in. When used for large groups, the size of the image can be regulated by changing the distance between the reader and the screen.

Home study. Home study, in the form of continuing education, correspondence courses, and home teaching for students with lengthy illnesses, is a "natural" for microforms. Distribution of the lesson and enrichment material in microform can be quite economical. Low cost, portable microform readers are available which can be loaned or rented by the school to the student. Or, the student may wish to obtain one personally.

Handicapped students. For students with visual difficulties, microform images can be projected larger than normal by using an appropriate lens. Experimentation with various sized lenses will help to determine which size image is best for each visually impaired student. This capability can also be used for slow readers. For children with dyslexia (reading dysfunction), microforms can also be useful.

Some physically handicapped students find that they can use microforms when it may be impossible to use hard copy. Microform readers can be modified to respond to remote control devices operated by any movable part of the body. For bedridden or disabled persons, materials can be projected on a screen or on a horizontal surface.

Remedial education. Microforms have particular application with students who need special help to sharpen specific skills. They can be assigned work which will help correct the deficiency, and work can be studied at the students' own speed. A student-tutor could be utilized to assist the students doing remedial work. By projecting microform images on paper on a table, children can trace, complete tasks, do calculations, draw, color, etc.

Foreign students, needing special help with language skills, can be helped by the use of microforms. For example, bilingual material can be acquired, with the material arranged on the film in such a way that both languages will appear on the microform reader screen side-by-side for comparison. Bilingual exercises can be presented in programmed fashion using microfiche.

Methods of Using Microforms

Fiche/text. A useful method of incorporating microforms into the teaching/learning program is to combine the strengths of microfiche and hardcopy printed or graphic material. Some examples may be useful.

1. **Fiche/books.** To include color plates in books (art, science, etc.) is expensive. Some presses are meeting the challenge of rising costs by including only the textual material in the book and referring the reader to a color microfiche for the pictorial information (see Figure 22). This color microfiche, much less costly to produce, can be included in a special pocket or holder in the book itself. Hence, the student sits at a microfiche reader while studying, referring to the color image when directed by the text.

2. **Fiche/workbook.** In this mode, the student reads or views the basic class or unit material on the microfiche and then works problems or does completion tasks by hand in an accompanying workbook.

3. **Fiche/flip chart.** The student follows the written instructions as he or she reads the material on the fiche and then refers to the graphic material on the flip chart.

Fiche/tape. Another method of using fiche in a multimedia way, which is gaining in popularity, is the combination of microfiche and audio tape (see Figure 23). Using this combination, several approaches are possible.

1. **Individual study.** Using a headset to insure acoustical isolation, the student can move at his or her own pace. The fiche may contain illustrations of biology specimens, and the audio cassette may contain the explanation. The audio, which tells the student when to move to the next frame, may be

Figure 22

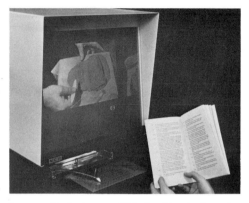

Pottery Techniques of Native North Americans,
part of the University of Chicago Press Text-Fiche Series

Figure 23

*Elementary School Student Doing Individual Work
with Microfiche and Audio Recording*

stopped at any time for a break or be rewound and replayed for review. If the student desires to study a particular frame longer than allowed for, he or she can stop the tape, study the illustration, then restart when desired. Of course, headsets are not necessary when studying is done in an area where no one would be distracted by the audio.

2. **Group learning.** Instead of using slides or a filmstrip with sound, try microfiche. As stated earlier, a microfiche reader can become a projector. The audio tape with audible signal can provide the sound and the instructions for advancing to the right frame of the fiche. A variation of this is for each student in a small group to have his or her own reader and fiche but only one cassette tape. In this situation, each student must remain alert to the signal so that he or she may keep the visual and the audio in synchronization. A multiple jack can be used to supply each student in the small group with a headset to insure acoustical isolation.

Reader used as a projector. A microfiche reader used as a projector (see Figure 24) offers considerable versatility. Some applications have been considered earlier and other specific uses follow; however, it seems appropriate to emphasize another aspect of educational uses of microforms here.

Today's teachers are expected to be much more mobile as well as more flexible in their methodologies. Microforms meet these demands. When a teacher who is a specialist in a given subject or skill is required to travel from room to room and even between schools, it is important for that teacher to be able to move with ease. Microfiche offers this possibility. A hypothetical case: A speech therapist is assigned from the district level to visit three schools in one day. The material he or she will present to the students at each elementary school is basically the same. This teacher has elected to project several vowel sounds on a screen, have the students repeat the sounds as a group, show the vowels in word context and then sentence context, assign the students to study these on their

Figure 24

A Microfiche Reader Being Used as a Projector

own, then re-drill them and test them. Instead of taking time to write all of these examples, exercises, and exams on a board or carry around many paper handouts, pieces of equipment, or large, cumbersome charts and visuals, the teacher has converted all of these to microfiche format. Now he or she simply places the necessary number of 4" x 6" sheets of microfiche in a briefcase and, upon arrival at the school, is ready to make a presentation in a matter of seconds. The microfiche reader with projection capabilities has been obtained, tested, and is ready for use upon arrival. The teacher moves from image to image at the pace most appropriate for the group with whom he or she is working. The teacher can pause, answer questions, elaborate, review, and test without the need for other, more expensive equipment. Copies of the fiche lesson material may be left with the students for study and drilling until the next visit. Using a reader/printer, a hardcopy print may be made of any image and left with a student needing assistance.

Use of Microforms in Specific Subjects

This section is included to highlight the use of microforms in specific applications. This is only a sampling, which hopefully will act as a catalyst to generating more ideas about ways in which microforms can be used.

Language arts. Microform copies of publications which date back to the 18th and 19th centuries give students the advantage of studying primary sources. These materials can give added insights about authors. Students can also read critical reactions to plays and books current at the time of production or publication.

Microform copies of newspaper and magazine ads are a rich source for drama students doing a unit on costume styles of a given era.

These primary sources are perfect for the study of language idioms, phrases, and words used in a specific time period.

When it comes to reading, teachers can project stories on a screen, and students can follow along as the teacher reads. Or, the students can take turns reading aloud. Group interpretations or explanations are conveniently done in this way.

The teaching of penmanship can be facilitated by projecting samples of letters, words, or sentences onto a piece of paper on the desk. The student then traces over the samples several times to get the feel of the strokes, then turns off the machine and tries it on his or her own.

Social studies. Studies of social issues are enhanced with non-textbook sources, such as microform copies of newspapers, magazines, and broadsides. Reading these materials can help to identify trends and to facilitate the tracing of those trends. Wage and price scales as well as job opportunities are excellent examples of this sort of study.

Art. Obtaining and maintaining a collection of art prints is often out of the scope of economic reality for some schools. However, microform copies of art work now make it possible for any school to afford such a resource. Collections of basic research material have become available at a fraction of the cost of printed originals. Just in the last few years, microfiche has exploded into the area of visual materials. With microfiche, school art departments can obtain art collections to use as reference materials. When projected, these art works are rich in color and sometimes are larger than the printed page of a text or the original work. Students can paint or trace from these reproductions (see Figure 25).

Business. Microforms offer a practical, hands-on way of teaching records management. Microforms are not the only means of storing and retrieving information in an office, but this is an important and increasing application. The way microforms and computers interact in business is a study of its own.

Again, the study of ads of companies can give an insight into the style of management, the history of the company, and how the company responds to social and economic trends of the nation. It is always interesting to deal specifically with the text of the ad itself. What about the length of the ad? How effective is a long ad? A short one? Is it too involved? What about the size of the words used? To what audience is the company speaking through its ads? Did the ads, or a specific ad, have any identifiable effect on the growth of the company? Comparing ads of similar products sold by different companies can sometimes be revealing. Tracing the pricing history of a given product or service can be valuable.

History. Microforms can play a significant role in the teaching of history. The typical history textbook quickly loses its luster after a student has been introduced to microform copies of the rich, original materials of the past.

Figure 25

*A Kindergarten Student Using a Portable Microfiche Reader
to Trace an Object Being Projected on a Sheet of Paper (Fuji RFP2)*

Past events seem to come alive when they are read in contemporary newspapers, journals, diaries, and letters. The originals of these kinds of materials are simply not available to elementary or secondary students. They are sometimes available with permission to the most serious researcher and scholar.

Imagine teaching a unit on the War of 1812. The student is given the assignment to research the War and write a report containing:

(1) a comparison of the coverage of a particular battle or event of the student's choice, as reported in newspapers of both sides;

(2) a personal account of one of the soldiers on either side as recorded in his journal or in letters written to family members; and

(3) a perspective from a leader's point of view as recorded in official correspondence or documents.

This is an excellent way of teaching the concept of objective study and research. It also adds a dimension of reality to an historical event. Some discretion will need to be used on the part of the teacher since, in this kind of research, the student can, on occasion, run into some raw language as an event is described.

Local history, so valuable in the education of a child, can be brought to life by projecting microform images of old records for children to read and discuss. Local college and universities and sometimes public libraries are depositories for materials which add light to local history. Rightfully, archivists and librarians are reluctant to allow the actual items to leave the safety of acid-free containers. However, through cooperative efforts, it may be possible to have some of the more representative items captured on microform for use in education. Examples of the type of material which will enhance local history include a handbill or poster advertising a theatrical production when a famous actor came to town; a "wanted" poster of a local "bad man"; a stagecoach ticket; a Confederate dollar; etc. The list is limited only by one's imagination.

Science. Through the use of microforms in teaching science, several advantages become apparent. As in other disciplines, students can study original papers of scientists. A concept in science may be traced from its earliest publication to the present.

In several areas of science, specimens become essential. Many science labs contain box after box of color slides and cabinets of microscopes. Microforms and microform readers can offer greater teaching flexibility at less cost than slides and microscopes. Microfiche can eliminate expensive slide sets, which are often difficult to handle and maintain. Because of the expense, it is difficult to have more than one set of specimens. With microfiche, any number of sets may be made at a minimal cost. Depending on the type of microscope and microfiche reader, it is possible to purchase readers at less cost than microscopes. A microfiche reader offers the further advantage of allowing the class and instructor to view a projected specimen together and to discuss it.

The quality of color microfiche, the ease of transporting (in-person or by mail), and the low cost of duplication make it ideal for specimens to be shared between schools, if necessary, as well as allowing the students to study them on their own in the school library or at home if they have readers.

Mathematics. In a unit on mathematics, in addition to all of the advantages listed earlier when used in other subjects, the student can do completion tasks. One example of this type of usage might be in learning multiplication tables. During individual study, the problem, without the answer, could be projected onto a piece of paper on the desk. The student could write his or her answer on the paper, move to the next frame, which contains the correct answer, and then compare. Story problems can be handled in the same manner.

10.

Future Educational Uses of Microforms

There are some discernible trends which will affect the educational use of microforms. At this point, one can safely say that most use of microforms in school is on an experimental basis. Comparatively few teachers have used them to date. The literature first begins to speak about the educational use of microforms in the mid-1960's. There is a noticeable increase of its mention in the literature from that point on, but the application of microforms in the teaching/learning process is still in its infancy.

Though in its beginning stages, momentum is building as educators discover the potential. This momentum on the part of education is putting pressure on two distinct areas: bibliographic control of microforms, and production of software and hardware more suitable to use for education both in schools and in the home.

A considerable amount of microfilming has taken place over the past three decades. Many micropublishers have produced millions of bibliographic units of material. Much of this has potential use in the schools. Some of it has been brought to the attention of teachers and librarians at the elementary and secondary level, but much of it has not been shown widely. Part of this is due to the lack of insight on the part of micropublishers as to the potential use of their product in this segment of the market. Part of the problem is caused by what is called poor bibliographic control of these materials. In other words, obscure trails are laid to them so that only the expert can find what is out there in micropublishing land. Both of these situations are changing. The micropublishers will produce collections and materials specifically for schools; will package them in such a way as to attract the educators' business; and will make certain that adequate bibliographic trails are provided. Librarians are making strides in the area of bibliographic control as well. What they are proposing and doing will make it easier for the teacher to discover what is already available.

The future will also bring more commercially produced multimedia teaching/learning systems using microforms, especially microfiche. These will appear in the form of hand- and automatic-advance, self-contained, sound/fiche systems, projection devices, and software packages requiring the use of more than one medium.

Equipment manufacturers will design and manufacture reading machines and associated equipment with school use in mind. These will be better adaptable to projection, and for use by the physically and mentally handicapped. Various sized lenses will assist those who have difficulty in reading. They will be designed for ease of portability by large and small students. They will be manufactured with even lighter-weight materials.

School supply stores will begin to stock these newly designed microform readers. We will see more readers in homes, taking their place as standard learning equipment alongside the cassette player and the home movie projector. This will escalate the use of microforms in home study courses and in continuing education.

The future of microform use in education is bright. The tip of the iceberg is just barely in sight. Only one's imagination will limit the possibilities. It is recognized that this book offers only a few ways in which this important medium can be used to better educate our students. It is hoped, however, that it will be used as a springboard to innovative and meaningful uses of microforms in the education process.

11.

Glossary

Archival quality. Refers to the ability of processed microform to retain its original characteristics during use and storage and to resist deterioration over time.

Camera, planetary (flat bed). A microfilm camera in which the source document is exposed while positioned on a flat copyboard or glass platen.

Camera, rotary (flow). A microfilm camera in which source documents are exposed as they rotate past a narrow slit aperture.

Camera, step and repeat. A microfilm camera which can expose a series of separate images on an area of film according to a predetermined format of rows and columns.

Cartridge. A single-core container for 16mm or 35mm microfilm. When mounted on an appropriate reader, microfilm from the cartridge is automatically threaded onto a take-up spool built into the reader.

Cassette. A double-core container for 16mm microfilm which encloses both a supply and take-up spool in a single housing.

Computer-output-microfilm. The end product of a process that converts machine-readable, digital data to eye-readable information on microform without first creating paper documents.

Diazo material. A slow print film or paper, sensitized by means of diazonium salts, which, subsequent to exposure to light strong in blue to ultraviolet spectrum, and development, forms an image.

Distribution copies. Microfilm copies, usually second or third generation, produced from camera microfilm or intermediates for distribution to the user.

Dry silver film. A non-gelatin film which is developed by the application of heat.

Duplicate microform. A microform created by duplicating an existing microform.

Generation. A measure of the remoteness of a particular microform from the original source document or computer output. The camera-original microform is a first-generation microform. A duplicate made from it is a second-generation, and so on.

Hand viewer. A small, portable magnifying device used for viewing microform. Magnification generally ranges from 5X to 15X.

Hard copy. An enlarged copy, usually on paper, of an image on microform.

Image. A representation of an object such as a document or other information sources produced by light rays.

Image rotation. A feature of a reader that enables the user to turn the displayed micro-image to compensate for the various positions of documents on film.

Microcard. An opaque microform, usually three by five inches in size, on which micro-images are affixed.

Microfiche. A sheet of microfilm containing multiple micro-images in a grid pattern. It usually contains a title which can be read without magnification. The term microfiche is both singular and plural.

Microfilm. A fine-grain, high-resolution film containing images greatly reduced in size from the original; used also as a verb to denote the recording of micro-images on film.

Microform. A generic term for any form, either film or paper, which contains micro-images.

Micrographics. A general term used to denote all activities relating to the creation or use of microforms.

Micro-image. A unit of information too small to be read without magnification.

Micro-opaque. A microform distinguished by a paper rather than a film image support.

Microprint. Trade-name for opaque microform created by the Readex Microprint Corporation. Microprint is created by printing reduced document images on rag content card stock.

Micropublishing. The production of information in multi-copy microform for sale or distribution to the public.

Polarity. A word used to indicate the change or retention of the dark to light relationship of an image.

Reader. A projection device that magnifies micro-images so they can be read with the unaided eye.

Reader/printer. A projection device that magnifies micro-images for screen display and prints paper enlargements of displayed images on user demand.

Reduction. A measure of the number of times a given linear dimension of an object is reduced when photographed, expressed as 14X, 24X, 48X, etc.

Reel. A flanged holder for wound microfilm.

Resolution. A measure of the ability of optical systems and photographic materials to render fine detail visible.

Roll microfilm. A generic term which encompasses microfilm on reels, in cartridges, and in cassettes.

Silver halide. A compound of silver and one of the known halogens: chlorine, bromine, iodine, or flourine.

Ultrafiche. Microfiche with images reduced more than 90X.

Vesicular film. Film which has the light-sensitive element suspended in a plastic layer and which upon exposure creates strains within the layer to form a latent image.

12.

Annotated Bibliography of Media About Microforms

Bridges to Inquiry. University Microfilms, 1979. Roll microfilm, plus student, teacher, and librarian manuals. Focusing on the social and behavioral sciences, this series contains selected microfilms which express periodical opinion in such areas as psychology, environment, urban problems, public welfare, and public education.

ERIC: What It Is, How to Use It. U.S. Educational Resources Information Center, 1974. Sound. Color. Three filmstrips, plus coordinator's manual and demonstration mock-ups. This kit is designed to teach the use of ERIC materials. It is a basic introduction to this collection of educational materials; how to use *Research in Education*; and the search process itself.

A Microcourse in Microform: An Instructional Program on Microfilm and Microfiche Readers and Printers. University Microfilms International, 1978. 10 min. Sound. Color, 16mm cartridge filmstrip plus printed guide. Also available in 35mm slides. An educational package in layman's language that introduces the student to microfilm, microfiche, and microform readers and reader/printers as well as to the wealth of information which this format can provide. It is a self-help tool on how to operate the equipment through step-by-step demonstrations. Also taught is where to find information in microform, how to access it, and how to handle it.

Micrographic Training Package. National Micrographics Association, 1978. Sound. Color. Microfiche and printed booklets. Aimed at the technician and others, this multimedia instruction package is designed to improve the knowledge level about micrographic methods, techniques, formats, and terms. Subjects covered include black and white films, color films, processing, quality control, duplication, and printing.

13.

Selected Bibliography of Micrographics

Beck, William L. "A Realistic Approach to Microform Management," *Microform Review,* 2:172-176 (1973).

Boni, Albert. "Readex Microprint: How It Began," *Microdoc,* 11:5-10 (1972).

Brunet, Lise. "JULIE: A Response to the Information Needs of Teachers of Maladjusted Children," *Educational Documentation and Information,* 17-2 (3rd Quarter, 1974).

Burchinal, Lee G. "Uses of Microfilm in Educational Institutions," *The Journal of Micrographics,* 7:107-112 (Jan. 1974).

Christine, Emma Ruth. "Microfilm in the Curriculum at Henry M. Gunn High School," *The Journal of Micrographics,* 5:141-145 (Jan. 1972).

Cohen, Abraham J. "The Use of Microfilm in the White Plains, N.Y. Public Schools," *The Journal of Micrographics,* 7:3-7 (Sept. 1973).

Darling, Pamela. "Microforms in Libraries: Preservation and Storage," *Microform Review,* 5:93-100 (1976).

Deline, Nancy E. "Microforms in the Secondary School," *Canadian Library Journal,* 34:175-179 (June 1977).

Douglas, Dan. "Small Beginnings," *Times (London) Educational Supplement,* No. 3178:63 (April 30, 1976).

Fair, Judy. "The Microtext Reading Room: A Practical

Approach," *Microform Review,* 1:199-203, 269-273 (1972), 2:9-13 (1973).

Finklestein, Norman H. "Gone Fiching," *Audiovisual Instruction,* 22:41 (Sept. 1977).

Fothergill, Richard. "Microfiche in Education Settings," *Educational Media International,* No. 2:2-7 (1976).

Fothergill, Richard. "Small Is Beautiful," *Times (London) Educational Supplement,* No. 3284:52 (June 9, 1978).

Gabriel, Michael R. *Micrographics, 1900-1977 A Bibliography* (Mankato, Minnesota Scholarly Press, 1978).

Goldberg, Martin M. "An Overview of Microfilm," *Audiovisual Instruction,* 22:44-45 (Sept. 1977).

Grausnick, Robert R. *et al. Microform Use in a Technical Training Environment: An Experiment. Final Report.* Denver: Denver University, Colorado Research Institute, May 1971, ED 056 484.

Grausnick, Robert, and Kottenstette, James P. *An Investigation of the Environment for Educational Microform Utilization. Phase 1, Student Use of Classroom Microform in Support of a Survey Course.* Denver: Denver University, Colorado Research Institute, April 30, 1971, ED 050 602.

Gregory, Roma S. "Acquisition of Microforms," *Library Trends,* 18:373-384 (1970).

Guide to Microforms in Print. Westport, CT: Microform Review, 1976–.

Hanson, L.E., and Rhodes, H.E. "Color Microfiche Strengthen Veterinary Courses," *Audiovisual Instruction,* 18:34, 36 (Oct. 1973).

Harmon, Catherine, and Harmon, George. *Microfilm in the Classroom: The Barrington School Project.* Silver Spring, MD: National Microfilm Association, 1971.

Harmon, George H. "Is Microform Ready for Classroom Use?" *The Journal of Micrographics,* 5:257-260 (1972).

Hein, Kathleen M. "The Role of Microforms in the Small College Library," *Microform Review,* 3:254-259 (1974).

Holmes, Donald C. *Determination of the Environmental Conditions Required in a Library for the Effective Utilization of Microforms.* Washington, D.C.: Office of Education, Bureau of Research, 1970.

Horder, Alan. "The Application of Microforms in Education: A Survey of the Literature," *British Journal of Educational Technology,* 6:38-54 (Jan. 1975).

Horder, Alan. "Finding More Colourful Uses for Microfiche," *Times Higher Education Supplement,* No. 326:13 (Feb. 3, 1978).

Kottenstette, James P. *et al. A Guide to Instructional Uses of Microform, Final Report.* Denver: Denver University, Colorado Research Institute, May 1971, ED 056 485.

Kottenstette, James P., and Dailey, K. Anne. *An Investigation of the Environment for Educational Microform Utilization. Phase II. Student Use of Classroom Microform in Support of a Content Course.* Denver: Denver University, Colorado Research Institute, April 30, 1971, ED 050 603.

Lagace, Robert L. *Nature and Uses of the HRAF Files: A Research Teaching Guide.* New Haven, CT: Human Relations Area Files, Inc., 1974.

Lee, Leonard S. "Speak Softly But Carry a Big Fiche," *The Journal of Micrographics,* 7:185-187 (1974).

Lee, Thomas Graham. *Current Trends in Microform Use by Secondary Schools, Four Case Studies,* ERIC, June 1969, ED 033 264.

Lee, Thomas Graham. *Microform Systems: A Handbook for Educators.* Ann Arbor: Michigan Audio-Visual Association, 1970.

Lewis, Ralph W. "User's Reaction to Microfiche: A Preliminary Study," *College and Research Libraries,* 31:260-268 (1970).

Logie, Audrey. "Access to Readex Microprint U.S. Government Depository Collection," *Government Publications Review,* 2:102-110 (1975).

Lynden, Frederick C. "Replacement of Hard Copy by Microforms," *Microform Review,* 4:9-14 (1975).

Maxin, Jacqueline A. "The Open Shelving of Journals on Microfilm," *Special Libraries,* 66:592-594 (1975).

"Microfiche Helps Students in Making Their Choice of Careers and Training," *Industrial Education,* 65:74 (Nov. 1976).

Microform Review. Westport, CT: Microform Review, Inc., 1972–.

Microforms in Libraries: A Reader. Edited by Albert J. Diaz. Westport, CT: Microform Review, Inc., 1975.

Micropublishers' Trade List Annual. Westport, CT: Microform Review, Inc., 1975–.

Mohammad, Abdel Rahim. "Microfiche Cards: An Approach in the Teaching of Laboratory Oral Histology and Oral Pathology," *International Journal of Instructional Media,* 4:87-90 (1976-77).

Nitsos, James L. "You're Buying a Micro-What?" *Audiovisual Instruction,* 22:20-21 (Oct. 1976).

Nutter, Susan K. "Microforms and the User: Key Variables of User Acceptance in a Library Environment," *Drexel Library Quarterly,* 11:17-31 (1975).

Reichmann, Felix, and Thorpe, Josephine. *Bibliographic Control of Microforms.* Westport, CT: Greenwood Press, 1972.

Reno, Edward A., Jr. "Some Basic Aspects of Scholarly Micropublishing," *Proceedings of the National Microfilm Association.* Silver Springs, MD: National Microfilm Association, 1973.

Repp, Joan M. "Microforms in the Elementary School: Problems and Promises," *The Journal of Micrographics,* 8:115-120 (Jan. 1975).

Rice, E. Stevens. *Fiche and Reel.* Ann Arbor: University Microfilms International, 1977.

Robbins, A.X. "Which Is It? Education or Learning? *The Journal of Micrographics,* 4:101-104 (Jan. 1971).

Rothschild, Eric. "Microfilm in Secondary Education," *The Journal of Micrographics*, 4:105-111 (Jan. 1971).

Saffady, William. *Micrographics*. Littleton, CO: Libraries Unlimited, Inc., 1978.

Smith, Chandler. "Color Microfiche for Teaching Anatomic Pathology," *The Journal of Micrographics*, 4:83-89 (Jan. 1971).

Spaulding, Carl. "Teaching the Use of Microfilm Readers," *Microform Review*, 6:80-81 (1977).

Spreitzer, Francis. "Library Microform Facilities," *Library Technology Reports*, 12:407-436 (1976).

Teague, J. "Microform: A Developing Medium," *New Library World*, 76:119-122 (1975).

Veaner, A.B. *The Evaluation of Micropublications: A Handbook for Librarians*. Chicago: American Library Association, 1971.

Veaner, A.B. "Microfilm and the Library: A Retrospective," *Drexel Library Quarterly*, 11:3-16 (1975).

Veaner, A.B. "Microproduction and Micropublication Standards: What They Mean to You, the User," *Microform Review*, 3:80-84 (1975).

Veitz, Fritz. "Microforms, Microform Equipment, and Microform Use in the Educational Environment," *Library Trends*, 19:447-466 (1971).

14.

Microform Equipment Manufacturers

Duplicators

Bell & Howell
Business Equipment Group
6800 McCormick Road
Chicago, Illinois 60645

Blue-Ray, Incorporated
P.O. Box 337
Essex, Connecticut 06426

Bruning
Division of Addressograph-Multi-
    graph
1555 Times Drive
Des Plaines, Illinois 60018

Eastman Kodak Company
Business Products Division
343 State Street
Rochester, N.Y. 14650

Micobra Corporation
176 King Street
Hanover, Massachusetts 02339

3M Company
Microfilm Products Division
3M Center
St. Paul, Minnesota 55101

Exposure Units, Vesicular

Canon (USA), Incorporated
10 Nevada Drive
Lake Success, N.Y. 11040

DASA Corporation
15 Stevens Street
Andover, Massachusetts 01810

Metro-Kalver, Incorporated
745 Post Road
Darien, Connecticut 06820

Micobra Corporation
176 King Street
Hanover, Massachusetts 02339

3M Company
Microfilm Products Division
3M Center
St. Paul, Minnesota 55101

Developers, Diazo

Bell & Howell
Business Equipment Group
6800 McCormick Road
Chicago, Illinois 60645

Blue-Ray, Incorporated
P.O. Box 337
Essex, Connecticut 06426

Bruning
Division of Addressograph-Multigraph
1555 Times Drive
Des Plains, Illinois 60018

Canon (USA), Incorporated
10 Nevada Drive
Lake Success, N.Y. 11040

DASA Corporation
15 Stevens Street
Andover, Massachusetts 01810

Eastman Kodak Company
Business Products Division
343 State Street
Rochester, N.Y. 14650

Micobra Corporation
176 King Street
Hanover, Massachusetts 02339

3M Company
Microfilm Products Division
3M Center
St. Paul, Minnesota 55101

Developers, Vesicular

Canon (USA), Incorporated
10 Nevada Drive
Lake Success, N.Y. 11040

Metro-Kalvar, Incorporated
745 Post Road
Darien, Connecticut 06820

Micobra Corporation
176 King Street
Hanover, Massachusetts 02339

3M Company
Microfilm Products Division
3M Center
St. Paul, Minnesota 55101

Inspection Stations, 16/35mm

Bell & Howell
Business Equipment Group
6800 McCormick Road
Chicago, Illinois 60645

Prestoseal Manufacturing Corpo-
  ration
P.O. Box 672
Flushing, N.Y. 11352

3M Company
Microfilm Products Division
3M Center
St. Paul, Minnesota 55101

Inspection Stations, Microfiche

HF Photo Systems, Incorporated
11801 West Olympic Boulevard
Los Angeles, California 90064

Readers, 16mm, Portable

Realist, Incorporated
P.O. Box 67
Menomonee Falls, Wisconsin
53051

Readers, 16mm, Table-top

Bell & Howell
Business Equipment Group
6800 McCormick Road
Chicago, Illinois 60645

Canon (USA), Incorporated
10 Nevada Drive
Lake Success, N.Y. 11040

DuKane Corporation
3145 North 11th Avenue
St. Charles, Illinois 60174

Eastman Kodak Company
Business Products Division
343 State Street
Rochester, N.Y. 14650

University Microfilms
300 North Zeeb Road
Ann Arbor, Michigan 48103

Readers, Rollfilm, Portable 35mm

Realist, Incorporated
P.O. Box 67
Menomonee Falls, Wisconsin
53051

Readers, Rollfilm, 35mm Table-top

DuKane Corporation
3145 North 11th Avenue
St. Charles, Illinois 60174

Eastman Kodak Company
Business Products Division
343 State Street
Rochester, N.Y. 14650

Information Design
3247 Middlefield Road
Menlo Park, California 94025

University Microfilms
300 North Zeeb Road
Ann Arbor, Michigan 48103

Readers, Cartridge, Table-top

Bell & Howell
Business Equipment Group
6800 McCormick Road
Chicago, Illinois 60645

Information Handling Services
5500 South Valencia Way
Englewood, Colorado 80110

Readers, Microfiche, Portable

Bell & Howell
Business Equipment Group
6800 McCormick Road
Chicago, Illinois 60645

Canon (USA), Incorporated
10 Nevada Drive
Lake Success, N.Y. 11040

DASA Corporation
15 Stevens Street
Andover, Massachusetts 01810

Eastman Kodak Company
Business Products Division
343 State Street
Rochester, N.Y. 14650

Realist, Incorporated
P.O. Box 67
Menomonee Falls, Wisconsin
53051

Readers, Microfiche, Table-top

Bell & Howell
Business Equipment Group
6800 McCormick Road
Chicago, Illinois 60645

Bruning
Division of Addressograph-Multigraph
1555 Times Drive
Des Plaines, Illinois 60018

Canon (USA), Incorporated
10 Nevada Drive
Lake Success, N.Y. 11040

DASA Corporation
15 Stevens Street
Andover, Massachusetts 01810

Datagraphix
P.O. Box 2449
San Diego, California 92112

DuKane Corporation
3145 North 11th Avenue
St. Charles, Illinois 60174

Eastman Kodak Company
Business Products Division
343 State Street
Rochester, N.Y. 14650

GAF Corporations
140 West 51 Street
New York, N.Y. 10020

Micro Information Systems, Incorporated
467 Armour Circle N.E.
Atlanta, Georgia 30324

Realist, Incorporated
P.O. Box 67
Menomonee Falls, Wisconsin
53051

University Microfilms
300 North Zeeb Road
Ann Arbor, Michigan 48103

Readers, Ultrafiche

Library Resources, Incorporated
301 East Erie Street
Chicago, Illinois 60611

Microform Data Systems, Incorporated
2700 Sand Hill Road
Menlo Park, California 94025

NCR
1000 Cox Plaza
Dayton, Ohio 45439

Reader, Micro-opaque

NCR
1000 Cox Plaza
Dayton, Ohio 45439

Readex Microprint Corporation
101 Fifth Avenue
New York, N.Y. 10003

Splicing/Editing Equipment

Bell & Howell
Business Equipment Group
6800 McCormick Road
Chicago, Illinois 60645

DuPage Metal Products, Incorporated
211 South Main Street
Lombard, Illinois 60148

Eastman Kodak Company
Business Products Division
343 State Street
Rochester, N.Y. 14650

Kalvar Corporation
909 South Broad Street
New Orleans, Louisiana 70125

Neumade Products Corporation
720 White Plains Road
Scarsdale, N.Y. 10583

Prestoseal Manufacturing Corpo-
ration
P.O. Box 672
Flushing, N.Y. 11352

3M Company
Microfilm Products Division
3M Center
St. Paul, Minnesota 55101

Storage Cabinets, Rollfilm

Bell & Howell
Business Equipment Group
6800 McCormick Road
Chicago, Illinois 60645

Bretford Manufacturing Company
9715 Soreng Avenue
Schiller Park, Illinois 60176

Eastman Kodak Company
Business Products Division
343 State Street
Rochester, N.Y. 14650

Neumade Products Corporation
720 White Plains Road
Scarsdale, N.Y. 10583

3M Company
Microfilm Products Division
3M Center
St. Paul, Minnesota 55101

University Microfilms
300 North Zeeb Road
Ann Arbor, Michigan 48103

H. Wilson Corporation
555 West Taft Drive
South Holland, Illinois 60473

**Storage Cabinets, Cartridge/Cas-
sette**

Neumade Products Corporation
720 White Plains Road
Scarsdale, N.Y. 10583

3M Company
Microfilm Products Division
3M Center
St. Paul, Minnesota 55101

Wright Line
160 Gold Star Boulevard
Worcester, Massachusetts 01606

Storage Cabinets, Microfiche

Dexion, Incorporated
39-27 59th Street
Woodside, N.Y. 11377

Reader/Printers, Rollfilm

Bell & Howell
Business Equipment Group
6800 McCormick Road
Chicago, Illinois 60645

Canon (USA), Incorporated
10 Nevada Drive
Lake Success, N.Y. 11040

DASA Corporation
15 Stevens Street
Andover, Massachusetts 01810

Datagraphix
P.O. Box 2449
San Diego, California 92112

Eastman Kodak Company
Business Products Division
343 State Street
Rochester, N.Y. 14650

Micro Information Systems, Incorporated
467 Armour Circle N.E.
Atlanta, Georgia 30324

OCE-Elliott, Incorporated
6500 North Lincoln Avenue
Lincolnwood, Illinois 60645

3M Company
Microfilm Products Division
3M Center
St. Paul, Minnesota 55101

Xerox Business Products
Xerox Square
Rochester, N.Y. 14644

Reader/Printers, Cartridges

Bell & Howell
Business Equipment Group
6800 McCormick Road
Chicago, Illinois 60645

Eastman Kodak Company
Business Products Division
343 State Street
Rochester, N.Y. 14650

Micro Information Systems, Incorporated
467 Armour Circle N.E.
Atlanta, Georgia 30324

3M Company
Microfilm Products Division
3M Center
St. Paul, Minnesota 55101

Reader/Printers, Microfiche

Bell & Howell
Business Equipment Group
6800 McCormick Road
Chicago, Illinois 60645

Bruning
Division of Addressograph-Multigraph
1555 Times Drive
Des Plaines, Illinois 60018

Datagraphix
P.O. Box 2449
San Diego, California 92112

DuKane Corporation Communications Systems Division
3145 North 11th Avenue
St. Charles, Illinois 60174

Eastman Kodak Company
Business Products Division
343 State Street
Rochester, N.Y. 14650

Kalvar Corporation
909 South Broad Street
New Orleans, Louisiana 70125

Micro Information Systems, Incorporated
467 Armour Circle N.E.
Atlanta, Georgia 30324

OCE-Elliott, Incorporated
6500 North Lincoln Avenue
Lincolnwood, Illinois 60645

3M Company
Microfilm Products Division
3M Center
St. Paul, Minnesota 55101

Xerox Business Products
Xerox Square
Rochester, N.Y. 14644

15.

Microform Software Suppliers

Envelopes, Microfiche

Hollinger Corporation
3810-B South Four Mile Run
　　Drive
Arlington, Virginia 22206

NCR
1000 Cox Plaza
Dayton, Ohio 45439

U.S. Envelope Company
2001 Industry Avenue
Springfield, Massachusetts 01101

Visu-Flex Company
633 South Carondolet Street
Los Angeles, California 90057

Film, Duplicating, Diazo, Sheet

Bell & Howell
Business Equipment Group
6800 McCormick Road
Chicago, Illinois 60645

Bruning
Division of Addressograph-Multi-
　　graph
1555 Times Drive
Des Plaines, Illinois 60018

Keuffel and Esser Company
20 Whippany Road
Morristown, New Jersey 07960

Remington Rand
Office Systems Division
P.O. Box 171
Marietta, Ohio 45750

Scott Graphics
Holyoke, Massachusetts 01040

Xidex Corporation
305 Soquel Way
Sunnyvale, California 94086

**Film, Duplicating, Vesicular,
　　Sheet**

Datagraphix
P.O. Box 2449
San Diego, California 92112

Kalvar Corporation
907 South Broad Street
New Orleans, Louisiana 70125

Remington Rand
Office Systems Division
P.O. Box 171
Marietta, Ohio 45750

Xidex Corporation
305 Soquel Way
Sunnyvale, California 94086

U.S. Microfilm Sales Corporation
235 Montgomery Street
San Francisco, California 94104

Film Cleaners, Chemical

HF Photo Systems, Inc.
Division of Technology, Inc.
11801 West Olympic Boulevard
Los Angeles, California 90064

Jack C. Coffey Company
P.O. Box 131
Waukegan, Illinois 60085

Neumade Products Corporation
720 White Plains Road
Scarsdale, New York 10583

Film Cleaners, Dry Process

Simco, Incorporated
920 Walnut Street
Landsale, Pennsylvania 19446

Reels

Goldberg Brothers, Incorporated
3535 Larimer Street
Denver, Colorado 80205

Plastic Reel Corporation of
    America
Subsidiary of Williamhouse Re-
    gency, Inc.
640 South Commercial Avenue
Carlstadt, New Jersey 07072

Tayloreel Corporation
185 Murray Street
Rochester, New York 14606

16.

Selected List of Micropublishers

Academic Microforms, Inc.
1317 Filbert St.
Philadelphia, PA 19107

American Chemical Society
Microform Program
1155 Sixteenth St., N.W.
Washington, DC 20036

AMS Press, Inc.
56 East 13th St.
New York, NY 10003

Arthur H. Clark Company
1264 South Central Ave.
Glendale, CA 91024

Bay Microfilm, Inc.
737 Loma Verde Ave.
Palo Alto, CA 94303

Chemical Abstracts Service
P.O. Box 3012
Columbus, OH 43210

Congressional Information Service, Inc.
7101 Wisconsin Ave.
Washington, DC 20014

ERIC Document Reproduction
Service
P.O. Box 190
Arlington, VA 22210

The Frederic Luther Company
P.O. Box 20224
2803 East 56th Street
Indianapolis, IN 46220

General Microfilm Co.
(and Erasmus Press)
100 Inman St.
Cambridge, MA 02139

Greenwood Press
Microfilm Dept.
51 Riverside Ave.
Westport, CT 06880

Hoover Institution
Stanford University
Stanford, CA 94305

Human Relations Area Files
P.O. Box 2054, Yale Station
755 Prospect St.
New Haven, CT 06520

Information Design, Inc.
3247 Middlefield Road
Menlo Park, CA 94025

Information Handling Services
(Library & Education Service)
15 Inverness Way
Englewood, CO 80110

John Wiley & Sons, Inc.
605 Third Avenue
New York, NY 10016

Johnson Associates, Inc.
P.O. Box 1017
321 Greenwich Ave.
Greenwich, CT 06830

KTO Microform
Rte. 100
Millwood, NY 10546

Library Microfilms
737 Loma Verde Ave.
Palo Alto, CA 94303

Library Resources, Inc.
425 N. Michigan Avenue
Chicago, IL 60611

Los Angeles Times
Times Mirror Square
Los Angeles, CA 90053

Lost Cause Press
750-56 Starks Bldg.
Louisville, KY 40202

Micro Photo Division
Bell & Howell Company
Old Mansfield Road
Wooster, OH 44691

Microfilming Corporation
   of America
21 Harristown Rd.
Glen Rock, NJ 07452

Microform Review, Inc.
520 Riverside Avenue
P.O. Box 405
Saugatuck Station
Westport, CT 06880

Microforms International
   Marketing Corp.
(Subsidiary of Pergamon Press)
Fairview Park
Elmsford, NY 10523

National Micrographics
   Association
8728 Colesville Road
Silver Spring, MD 20910

NTIS (National Technical
   Information Service)
U.S. Dept. of Commerce
5285 Port Royal Rd.
Springfield, VA 22161

Readex Microprint Corporation
101 5th Avenue
New York, NY 10003

Research Publications, Inc.
12 Lunar Drive
Woodbridge, CT 06525

Scholarly Resources, Inc.
1508 Pennsylvania Avenue
Wilmington, DE 19806

University Microfilms
300 North Zeeb Road
Ann Arbor, MI 48103
(or)
University Microfilms International
18 Bedford Row
London WC1R 4EJ
England

About the Author

E. Dale Cluff is Director of Library Services, Southern Illinois University-Carbondale. He worked as a reference, order, and media librarian and as Assistant Director of Libraries at the University of Utah prior to his move to Illinois in January, 1980. Dr. Cluff has a Ph.D. in Educational Administration, a M.Lib. in Librarianship, and a B.A. in English. Professional activities include chairperson of Reproduction of Library Materials Section, member of the Micropublishing Committee (ALA), and President of Utah Library Association. Publications include annual review articles for *Library Resources and Technical Services* on developments in copying, micrographics, and graphic communications.